kick the clouds

**The Haiku Foundation
Volunteer Anthology 2025**

Edited by

Marta Chocilowska & Robert Kania

kick the clouds

*With gratitude to our wonderful volunteers —
we couldn't do it without you!*

Robin Smith
President

INTRODUCTION

Welcome to The Haiku Foundation's annual Volunteer Anthology, *Kick the Clouds*, our fourth such collection. This time, we're featuring the volunteers of the past three years who've given so freely of their time and expertise. The Board of Directors deeply appreciates their unwavering show of support and dedication during the past few years.

Marta Chocilowska chose the theme "back to childhood," which ties in well with the brief moments conveyed in haiku. We hope you enjoy reading through this edition where you'll not only encounter snippets of childhood but also get better acquainted with THF volunteers.

My sincere thanks to co-editors Marta Chocilowska and Robert Kania for their work gathering the poems and compiling this year's anthology. I would be remiss if I didn't thank THF's President, Robin Smith, for her invaluable assistance on tech issues and various editorial details. And kudos to Jacob Salzer, book setter extraordinaire, for his excellent work in bringing this publication to fruition.

— Theresa A. Cancro
THF Volunteer Appreciation Chair
Member, The Haiku Foundation Board of Directors

EDITOR'S PREFACE

Growing up is a unique journey — one moment you're a carefree child, and before you know it, you've stepped into adulthood. We've all experienced this transition, which brings both joy and nostalgia.

Robert and I believed that the theme of "back to childhood" might encourage our authors to open up and share their vulnerabilities. We were optimistic that this would resonate well and allow the poets to express themselves freely, and thankfully, it did! The nearly 100 poems in this collection showcase a wonderful variety of experiences — some joyful, some melancholic, and some a bit painful — and beautifully capture memories of people, places, objects, smells, and tastes in all their richness. We had a great time reading each poem, and we're truly grateful for the trust placed in us.

The theme is perfectly tied to the volume's title, inspired by a lovely line from Adelaide B. Shaw's haiku: "kick the clouds."

Let's take a moment to enjoy this shared journey into our childhood memories.

We sincerely thank Theresa A. Cancro and Robin Smith for their dedication and support, along with all the volunteers who made this anthology possible.

— Marta Chocilowska & Robert Kania
THF Volunteer Anthology Editors

• SUSAN ANTOLIN •

Walnut Creek, California, United States
Touchstone Distinguished Books Award Panelist

a jump rope song
half-remembered
summer afternoon

previously unpublished

• JEAN ANTONINI •

Lyon, France
Content Provider

vanilla ice cream
never had so many memories
of my youth

glace à la vanille—
jamais eu autant de souvenirs
de ma jeunesse

previously unpublished

• PAMELA A. BABUSCI •

Rochester, New York, United States

Content Provider

evening solitude . . .
hugging my childhood
teddy bear

Evergreen English Haiku, 2003

• DON BAIRD •

Wake Forest, North Carolina, United States
Site Administrator

red tricycle
the loneliness of a
playground

As the Crow Flies
Little Buddha Press, 2013

• ROBERTA BEARY •

Washington, D.C., United States /
Westport, County Mayo, Ireland
Roving Ambassador

merry-go-round
the moment dad
lets go

Modern Haiku 55.3

• NANCY BRADY •

Ohio, United States

Haiku Dialogue Guest Editor

first steps...
catching cherry blossoms
in chubby fist

Polish International Haiku Competition
2017, Honorary Mention

• SUSAN BURCH •

Hagerstown, Maryland, United States
Content Provider

risking it all floor M&M

previously unpublished

• SONDRA J. BYRNES •

New Mexico, United States
Content Provider

hide and seek
looking for the little girl
in me

failed haiku 33

• ROBYN CAIRNS •

Melbourne, Australia

Content Provider

forest picnic
searching for fairy rings
with my dad

previously unpublished

• DAN CAMPBELL •

Falls Church, Virginia, United States
Book of the Week Editor

remember how
we hovered, glided
and sometimes soared

THF Renku Sessions, November 2022

• THERESA A. CANCRO •

Wilmington, Delaware, United States

Managing Editor, *Haikupedia*

Board Member

bedtime story . . .
her teddy bear
approves

Brass Bell, December 2022

• ANTOINETTE CHEUNG •

Vancouver, British Columbia, Canada
Content Provider

braiding my doll's hair
the scent of oranges
from granny's fingers

First Frost, October 2022

• MARTA CHOCILOWSKA •

Warsaw, Poland

Haiku Registry Committee Chair

childhood blanket
now I wrap in it
my mother's chill

kocyk z dzieciństwa
teraz otulam nim chłód
mojej matki

cattails, May 2015

• MARION CLARKE •

Warrenpoint, Northern Ireland

Forum Administrator

rain clouds
a child speaks softly
to his kite

31st Indian Kukai, First Place

March 2020

• JOYCE CLEMENT •

Connecticut, United States

Touchstone Distinguished Books Award Panelist

milk bubbles
from a straw this universe
& that & that

Frogpond 38:2

• Cherie Hunter Day •

New Hampshire, United States

Content Provider

New Year's Day
my son lets the tide
seep into his sneakers

The Heron's Nest III, 5

• MELISSA DENNISON •

Bradford, West Yorkshire, United Kingdom
re:Virals Assistant Editor

pulling a face...
the taste of
mummy's lipstick

previously unpublished

• CHARLOTTE DIGREGORIO •

Winnetka, Illinois, United States
Publicity

in the red wagon
my brother and i bring home
our stiff cat

Frogpond 42:2

• DANIÈLE DUTEIL •

Bretagne, France
Content Provider

street hopscotch
the children have forgotten
the sky

marelle de rue
les enfants ont oublié
le ciel

previously unpublished

• ROBERT EPSTEIN •

El Cerrito, California, United States
Content Provider

children's cabin—
I hurry to unlock
the make-believe door

previously unpublished

• **KEITH EVETTS** •

Thames Ditton, United Kingdom
re:Virals Host & Managing Editor

the town canal
murky enough for a lad
to hope for a fish

Asahi Haikuist Network, June 6, 2025

• BRUCE H. FEINGOLD •

Berkeley, California, United States

Touchstone Awards Chair & Books Award Coordinator

Board Member

antique safe
granddad's yellowed, tattered
immigration papers

previously unpublished

• ANTONELLA FILIPPI •

Genova, Italy

Content Provider

dark cloud
the face of the moon
wears a moustache

previously unpublished

• P. H. FISCHER •

Vancouver, British Columbia, Canada

Haiku Dialogue Guest Editor

freeing the kite
i stay awhile
in the oak branches

A New Resonance 14
Red Moon Press, 2025

• LORIN FORD •

Brunswick, Victoria, Australia
Renku Sessions Sabaki

friend of seagulls
I dog-paddle out to their
warm sandbank

previously unpublished

• TERRI L. FRENCH •

Huntsville, Alabama, United States

Past Board Member

fairy tales
mother takes the edge
off the wolf

Prune Juice #39

• JENNIFER HAMBRICK •

Columbus, Ohio, United States

Content Provider

dandelion head games we play

Modern Haiku 53.2

• PENNY HARTER •

Mays Landing, New Jersey, United States
Archives Donor

my great aunt's parlor—
every visit my crayoned tulip
still stuck to the wall

previously unpublished

• JOHN HAWKHEAD •

Bradford on Avon, United Kingdom

Content Provider

picking broad beans
my father's earth-lined fingers
ruffling my hair

tsuri-dōrō #25

• MARILYN SHOEMAKER HAZELTON •

Allentown, Pennsylvania, United States
Content Provider

holding her crayons carefully
she draws herself and a friend
holding up the sun

previously unpublished

• GARY HOTHAM •

Scaggsville, Maryland, United States

Content Provider

after the nap—
the air pushed around
by the infant's hands

South by Southeast, 1999

• MARSHALL HRYCIUK •

Toronto, Canada

Renku Sessions Sabaki

first toy airplane
decals skidding
on its glue

previously unpublished

• EDWARD CODY HUDDLESTON •

Baxley, Georgia, United States

Touchstone Distinguished Books Award Panelist

dragon-shaped cloud
a boy names a stick
Excalibur

FiredUp Haiku

Bicadeideias Publishing, 2024

• LAKSHMI IYER •

Kerala, India

Content Provider

toddler's first glasses the silence

LEAF 3

• Jim Kacian •

Winchester, Virginia, United States
Chair of the Board of Directors

pilgrimage to a certain tree childhood

whiptail 14

• **ROBERT KANIA** •

Warsaw, Poland
Content Provider

first snow pierwszy śnieg
a little boy gets away chłopczyk wyrywa się
from his mother's arms z ramion matki

KUZU 3/2016 (Japanese version)

• DEBORAH KARL-BRANDT •

Sinzig, Germany

Haiku Dialogue Editor

trying harder
to exit the maze ...
board game night

previously unpublished

• ARVINDER KAUR •

Chandigarh, India

Haiku Dialogue Guest Editor

wicket gate
a path leads me
to a cicada's song

Frogpond 46:3

• JULIE BLOSS KELSEY •

Germantown, Maryland, United States

Board Member & Secretary

New to Haiku Coordinator & Content Provider

Pacific blues—
my childhood beach
lost to erosion

Haiku in Action

Week 8, Feb. 24, 2022

• KAT LEHMANN •

Guilford, Connecticut, United States
Touchstone Distinguished Books Award Panelist
Content Provider

eyes closing the aurora borealis as a child

previously unpublished

• MICHAEL H. LESTER •

California, United States

Content Provider

bare poplar
boys shooting marbles
on a patch of dirt

previously unpublished

• KRISTEN LINDQUIST •

Camden, Maine, United States

Touchstone Haibun Award Coordinator

revising my childhood
charred scraps of paper drift
from the burn barrel

Mayfly 74

• GREGORY LONGENECKER •

Pasadena, California, United States
Touchstone Award for Individual Poems Panelist

vacant lot
the kids find another
galaxy

The Heron's Nest XXII, 1

• PATRICIA J. MACHMILLER •

San Jose, California, United States

Renku Sessions Sabaki

lost pinwheel
the wind finds it
plays with it

Lost Pinwheel

YTHS Members' Anthology, 2019

• Carole MacRury •

Point Roberts, Washington, United States
Content Provider

doll house windows—
a spider spins a web
over my childhood

Samobor Susreti, 2019

• SCOTT MASON •

Somers, New York, United States

Board Member

first language
grandmother speaks
in yarn

Golden Haiku Poetry Competition

2025, Selected

• Marietta McGregor •

Canberra, Australia
Touchstone Award for Individual Haibun Panelist
Haiku Dialogue Guest Editor

backyard water games
a brother and sister leap
to split a rainbow

27th ITO EN Oi Ocha
New Haiku Contest, 2016
Merit Award

• DAVID MCMURRAY •

Maple Lake, Ontario, Canada
Content Provider

the white-spotted fawn
accepts the outstretched lily
from an open hand . . .

previously unpublished

• Beverly Acuff Momoi •

Mountain View, California, United States

Content Provider

summer of
the lunar landing
we grow wings

Origami Butterflies

YTHS Members' Anthology, 2024

• LENARD D. MOORE •

North Carolina, United States

Content Provider

severe weather—
I browse my scrapbook
from high school

previously unpublished

• JOANNE MORCOM •

Alberta, Canada

Content Provider

windy day
the hopscotch squares
fill with blossoms

Vancouver Cherry Blossom Festival

Haiku Invitational

Top Canada Winner, 2024

• Ron C. Moss •

Leslie Vale, Tasmania, Australia

Content Provider, HaikuLife Films

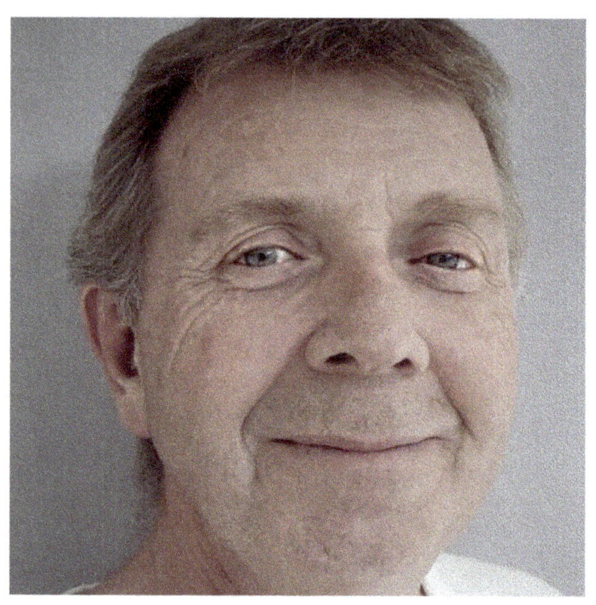

trolley derby race
i borrow the wheels
from my sister's pram

previously unpublished

• kjmunro •

Whitehorse, Yukon Territory, Canada

Haiku Dialogue Managing Editor

childhood innocence
giant soap bubbles
burst

The Solitary Daisy, Issue 50

• DAVID OATES •

Athens, Georgia, United States
Haiku of the Day Editor

finishes her candy bar—
even on her back,
chocolate

Drunken Robins
Brick Road Press, 2011

• **ELLEN GRACE OLINGER** •

Oostburg, Wisconsin, United States
Educational Content Provider

reading poetry
in the garden
summer school

Poems From Oostburg, Wisconsin

• VICTOR ORTIZ •

Bellingham, Washington, United States
Touchstone Distinguished Books Award Panelist

recess
children count
police cars

Roadrunner 6:3

• MAEVE O'SULLIVAN •

Dublin, Ireland
Content Provider

their raucous cries
echoing summer holidays—
kittiwakes

previously unpublished

• RENÉE OWEN •

Northern California, United States

Touchstone Award for Individual Haibun Panelist

name-calling
at the touch of a finger
a playground war

Marin Poetry Center Anthology XXI

• LORRAINE A PADDEN •

California, United States

Touchstone Awards Panelist (Books & Individual Haibun)

fledgling
her world from the top
of a swing

tsuri-dōrō #18

• Pravat Kumar Padhy •

Bhubaneswar, India

Touchstone Award for Individual Poems Panelist

swinging back and forth my childhood days

previously unpublished

• **JOHN PAPPAS** •

Boston, Massachusetts, United States

Content Provider

class reunion
the creak of
rusty swings

previously unpublished

• VANDANA PARASHAR •

Panchkula, India

Haiku Dialogue Guest Editor

unexpected showers
every puddle sets free
the child in me

Yamadera Basho Memorial Museum

English Haiku Contest, 2019, Selected

• CHRISTOPHER PATCHEL •

Philadelphia, Pennsylvania, United States

Touchstone Awards Panelist (Books & Individual Poems)

the bounce
of a rubber ball
brings it all back

Modern Haiku 44:2

• MARIANNE PAUL •

Kitchener, Ontario, Canada

Touchstone Award for Individual Poems Panelist

growing up poor
potatoes
and more potatoes

Brass Bell, May 2021

• STELLA PIERIDES •

Neusaess, Germany / London, United Kingdom

Past Board Member

Haiku for Parkinson's Coordinator

ripe seedhead
twisting and pulling
her milk teeth

previously unpublished

• MADHURI PILLAI •

Melbourne, Australia
Content Provider

replaying voices
in my head—
grandparents' house

previously unpublished

• **KALA RAMESH** •

Chennai, India
Content Provider

temple lotus
mother brings home
a smile

Acorn #46

• DIAN DUCHIN REED •

California, United States

Content Provider

her plastic pail
waiting by the bed
sand-dollar moon

tinywords 17.2

• **LYN REEVES** •

Tasmania, Australia

Content Provider

dollhouse—
behind each window
a perfect world

Echidna Tracks, March 2020

• BRYAN RICKERT •

Belleville, Illinois, United States

Content Provider

into the depths
of my childhood
this forest trail

previously unpublished

• VALÉRIE RIVOALLON •

Clichy, France

Events Calendar Editor

ocean of my childhood
on the other
planet ?

collective book *Mers...si*

Revidence 2025

• CHAD LEE ROBINSON •

South Dakota, United States

Touchstone Distinguished Books Award Panelist

first frost
a slight dent
in the tetherball

Acorn #12

• MICHELE ROOT-BERNSTEIN •

East Lansing, Michigan, United States
Haiku in English Editorial Team

my sister's side
of our childhood
moonlit night

The Heron's Nest XIII, 1

• CE ROSENOW •

Eugene, Oregon, United States

Juxtapositions Senior Editor

a new family
in my childhood home—
ebb tide

previously unpublished

• GABRIEL ROSENSTOCK •

Dublin, Ireland

Content Provider

chewing away - knowing nothing
but our name for them
'sour sallies'

previously unpublished

• Bona M. Santos •

Los Angeles, California, United States
Content Provider

the elusive sound
of my father's bamboo flute—
morning reverie

Southern California Haiku Study Group

Anthology 2022

• AGNES EVA SAVICH •

Austin, Texas, United States
Touchstone Award for Individual Poems Panelist

trying to give
advice to my daughter
wild rose bushes

Autumn Moon 7:2

• DAN SCHWERIN •

Sun Prairie, Wisconsin, United States

Touchstone Award for Individual Poems Panelist

the scrappy kid
recycling a five-cent bottle
for a death poem

bones 26

• JULIE SCHWERIN •

Sun Prairie, Wisconsin, United States
Content Provider

summer knights . . .
the field alight
with tiny dragons

Stardust Haiku #43

• SHLOKA SHANKAR •

Bangalore, India

Touchstone Award for Individual Poems Panelist

caught between Skip & Reverse family game night

previously unpublished

• ADELAIDE B. SHAW •

Somers, New York, United States
Content Provider

park swing
granddaughter and I
kick the clouds

previously unpublished

• NEENA SINGH •

Chandigarh, India

Content Provider

childhood home
I reach for a hand
no longer there

previously unpublished

• ROBIN SMITH •

Middletown, Delaware, United States

THF President

catching
a bruise on the boy
I should have been

Modern Haiku 53.3

• SHEILA SMITH MCKOY •

Raleigh, North Carolina, United States
Juxtapositions Editorial Board

wet spider web
above my treehouse
catbirds call

previously unpublished

• Maria Steyn •

Johannesburg, South Africa
Content Provider

year's end
her skipping rope
too short

The Heron's Nest III, 3

• ILIYANA STOYANOVA •

Leighton Buzzard, United Kingdom

Haikupedia Editor

doll party
another lump of mud
for the coffee

Igračke, 2017

• DEBBIE STRANGE •

Winnipeg, Manitoba, Canada

Content Provider

busker's hat
a child offers coins
of dried lunaria

Bloodroot Haiku Award 2022

First Place

• RICHARD STRAW •

Cary, North Carolina, United States
Former Digital Library Consultant

a long night
I repeat the prayers
of childhood

THF *Haiku Dialogue*, Jan. 8, 2025

• **Alan Summers** •

Chippenham, United Kingdom

Occasional Mentor

the skip in my step as I mentally unwrap wax paper sandwiches

previously unpublished

• GEORGE SWEDE •

Toronto, Ontario, Canada

Content Provider

abandoned homestead
against the fence
a divining rod

The Way A Poem Emerges
Lett Press, 2022

• MICHELLE TENNISON •

New Jersey, United States

Former Touchstone Awards Panelist

mother the slow rhythmic pulse of swan wings

Roadrunner 12.3

• CORINE TIMMER •

Faro, Portugal / The Netherlands

Content Provider

secret hideout—
my friend's smoke rings
better than mine

Blithe Spirit 32:4

• CHARLES TRUMBULL •

Santa Fe, New Mexico, United States

Haikupedia Editor-in-Chief

aged mother:
showing her how to do things
she taught me as a child

Wnosząc światło księżyca

Carrying Moonlight

International Haiku Conference

Kraków, Poland, 2003

• Toñi Sánchez Verdejo •

Albacete, Spain
Books Donor

the cherries' sweetness...
I take a handful of them
for my granny!

Little Red Riding Hood writes haiku

• MARILYN APPL WALKER •

Georgia, United States
Content Provider

an old love song
mother slices
home grown tomatoes

The Heron's Nest VI, 11

• JOHN ZHENG •

Mississippi, United States

Juxtapositions General Editor

childhood
a kite with a broken string
dives toward sea

previously unpublished